Cat Angels

Cat Angels

edited by
Jeff Rovin

illustrated by
Ernie Colon

HarperPaperbacks
A Division of HarperCollinsPublishers

HarperPaperbacks   *A Division of* HarperCollins*Publishers*
                10 East 53rd Street, New York, N.Y. 10022

Cover illustration by Kam Mak

Interior illustrations by Ernie Colon

First printing: November 1995

Printed in the United States of America

HarperPaperbacks and colophon are trademarks of
HarperCollins*Publishers*

Library of Congress Cataloging-in-Publication Data

Cat angels/edited by Jeff Rovin; illustrated by Ernie Colon.
    p. cm.
    ISBN 0-06-100972-5 (hardcover)
    1. Cats —poetry. 2. Cats—Quotations, maxims, etc.
    I. Rovin, Jeff.
PN6110.C3C35   1995
808.81'936—dc20   95-30925
                                              CIP

❖ 10 9 8 7 6 5 4 3 2 1

$\mathcal{G}$race and beauty, delicacy and gentleness, charisma and radiance, sweetness and strength.

These words apply not only to cats but to angels, the appointed messengers of God. And they apply to the wonderful union of the two, cat angels.

Historically, angels have been portrayed in different ways as they carry out the will and wishes of God. Some have staffs, some have wings of many colors. Some carry shields, others are pictured with swords, musical instruments, scrolls or scepters.

But as cats?

Although religious scholars have never said that angels can assume feline form, or that cats can be raised to such a lofty level, cat-owners have always known the truth:

Angels *can* be cats. And cats are angels, right here on earth, full of love and piety and even a sense of righteousness that humans find both wondrous and a little intimidating.

This book is a collection of quotes, poems, facts, and reflections about angelic cats and cat angels, about the passing of cats from this world to the next, about the odd cat ghost and curious winged cat, and about the immortal soul of the cat. There is somber prose by legendary authors, comic and occasionally irreverent thoughts from modern day humorists and celebrities, and light verse by both famous authors and those who are less well-known.

The author, artist, and editor hope you find these selections warm, amusing, and inspirational. For those of you who doubt that there *are* such things as cat angels, keep in mind this observation by the artist's four-year-old daughter Rebecca.

Upon hearing that cats aren't mentioned anywhere in the Bible, she looked up from her dinner plate and remarked, "That's because God gave them away as pets, to show us that He loves us."

And so He did.

Some say that cats are devils,
but they behave badly only when
they are alone. When they are
among us, cats are angels.

GEORGE SAND

Thou art the Great Cat, the avenger of the Gods, and the judge of words, and the president of the sovereign chiefs and the governor of the holy Circle.

Inscription on the
Royal Tombs at Thebes

$\mathcal{I}$f you gave wings to a cat, it would not condescend to be a bird. It would be an angel.

Dick Shawn

ST. PETER'S LAMENT

Peter said, "There is one thing I know'st,
Among cat angels highest and low'st.
They arrive, don their wings,
Then of all wicked things,
Use my gates as their new scratching post!"

Cats are very special angels, but they're
not angelic. Watch what happens when a
flock of birds fly by, beneath the clouds.

Elizabeth Hubbard Hall

*C*at angels are the reason
there are no mice angels.

Mel Brooks

$\mathcal{G}$od allows cats in Heaven just so
He can keep an eye on them.

Dixie Carter

A cat has a reputation to protect. If it had a halo, it would be worn cocked to one side.

WILL DURANT

In Istanbul, I met a man who said he knew beyond a doubt that God was a cat. I asked why he was so sure, and the man said, 'When I pray to him, he ignores me.'

LOWELL THOMAS

THE LITTLE CAT ANGEL

The ghost of a little white kitten
Crying mournfully, early and late,
Distracted St. Peter, the watchman,
As he guarded the heavenly gate.
"Say, what do you mean," said his saintship,
"Coming here and behaving like that?"
"I want to see Nellie, my missus,"
Sobbed the wee little ghost of a cat.
"I know she's not happy without me,
Won't you open and let me go in?"
"Begone," gasped the horrified watchman,
"Why the very idea is a sin;
I open the gate to good angels,
Not to stray little beggars like you."
"All right," mewed the little white kitten,
"Though a cat I'm a good angel, too."
Amazed at so bold an assertion,
But aware that he must make no mistake,
In silence, St. Peter long pondered,
For his name and repute were at stake,
Then placing the cat in his bosom
With a "Whist now, and say all your prayers,"
He opened the heavenly portals
And ascended the bright golden stairs.
A little girl angel came flying,
"That's my kitty, St. Peter," she cried.
And, seeing the joy in their meeting,
Peter let the cat angel abide.

This tale is the tale of a kitten
Dwelling now with the blessed above,
It vanquished grim Death and High Heaven
For the name of the kitten was Love.

Leontine Stanfield

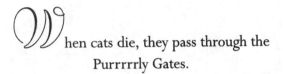

When cats die, they pass through the Purrrrrly Gates.

CATWOMAN

$\mathcal{N}$o heaven will not ever Heaven be
Unless my cats are there to welcome me.

EPITAPH IN A PET CEMETERY

In Memoriam –
Leo: A Yellow Cat

If to your twilight land of dream—
Persephone, Persephone,
Drifting with all your shadow host—
Dim sunlight comes, with sudden gleam
And you lift veiled eyes to see
Slip past a little golden ghost,
That wakes a sense of springing flowers,
Of nesting birds, and lambs newborn,
Of spring astir in quickening hours,
And young blades in Demeter's corn;
For joy of that sweet glimpse of sun,
O goddess of unnumbered dead,
Give one soft touch—if only one—
To that uplifted, pleading head!
Whisper some kindly word, to bless
A wistful soul who understands
That life is but one long caress
Of gentle words and gentle hands.

Margaret Sherwood

Leo to His Mistress

Dear Mistress, do not grieve for me
Even in such sweet poetry.
Alas! It is too late for that,
No mistress can recall her cat.
Eurydice remained a shade
Despite the music Orpheus played;
And pleasures here outlast, I guess,
Your earthly transitoriness.

You serious denizens of Earth
Know nothing of Elysian mirth;
With other shades I play or doze
And wash, and stretch, or rub my nose.
I hunt for mice, or take a nap
Safe in Iphigenia's lap.
At times I bite Achilles' heel
To learn if shadow heroes squeal,
And should he turn to do me hurt,
I hide beneath Cassandra's skirt.

But should he smile, no creature bolder,
I lightly bounce upon his shoulder,
Then leap to fair Electra's knee
Or scamper with Antigone.
I chase the rolling woolen ball
Penelope has just let fall,
And crouch when Meleager's cheer

Awakes the shades of trembling deer.
I grin when Stygian boys, beguiled,
Stare after Helen, Ruin's child;
Or should these placid pastimes fail
I play with Cerberus's tail.
At last I purr and spit and spatter
When kind Demeter fills my platter.

And yet, in spite of all of this,
I sometimes yearn for earthly bliss,
To hear you calling, "Leo!" when
The glorious sun awakens men;
Or hear your "Good night, Pussy" sound
When starlight falls on mortal ground;
Then, in my struggles to get free,
I almost scratch Persephone.

HENRY DWIGHT SEDGWICK

I believe cats to be spirits come to earth.
A cat, I am sure, could walk on a cloud
without coming through.

Jules Verne

*W*henever he was out of luck and a little
down-hearted, he would fall to mourning
over the loss of a wonderful cat he used to
own. . . . And he always spoke of the strange
sagacity of that cat with the air of a man
who believed in his secret heart that there
was something human about it—maybe
even supernatural.

MARK TWAIN

Not Quite

I once saw a kitty with wings on its back.
'Pussy,' said I, 'Are you angel or cat?'
Then I saw the rest of the bird by a shack.
And said to myself, 'Well, that answers that.'

ELAINE PAPA

Creatures
Angelic,
They.

Judy Burkow

A little drowsing cat is an image of perfect beatitude.

Champfleury

The cat passed on. In heaven by an
Angel he did sail.
Against the angel's harp he brushed, first
Cheek, then side, then tail.
The angel said, "Irrev'rence 'tis to
Pluck that, kitten. Shame!"
Not looking back, cat answered, "I am
Cat, and pluck's my name.

SHAY KAHRS

A cat has nine lives and nine souls,
and it must also have nine guardian angels
watching over it. Which would explain why
the little fellow is so smug.

Karen Fields-Hutton

As this nineteenth century poem suggests,
not all winged cats get to frolic in heaven.
And for such cats, having wings can pose—

A Serious Question

A kitten went a-walking
One morning in July,
And idly fell a-talking
With a great big butterfly.

The kitten's tone was airy,
The butterfly would scoff;
When there came along a fairy
Who whisked his wings right off.

And then,—for it is written
Fairies can do such things, —
Upon the startled kitten
She stuck the yellow wings.

The kitten felt a quiver,
She rose into the air,
Then flew down to the river
To view her image there.

With fear her heart was smitten,
And she began to cry:
"Am I a butter-kitten?
Or just a kitten-fly?"

Carolyn Wells

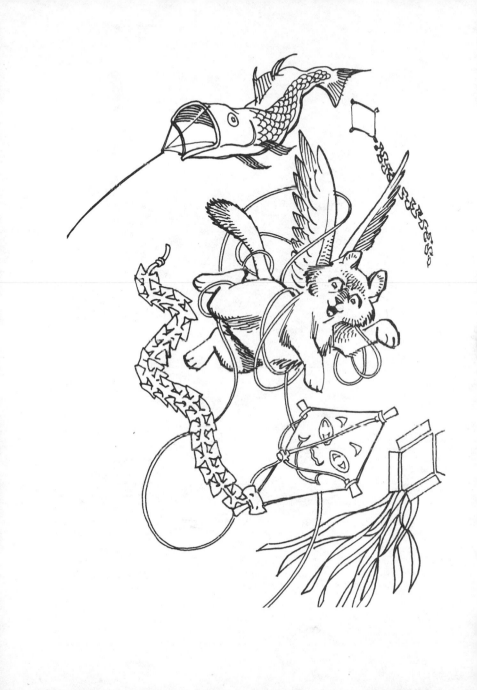

There once was a kitten with wings
Who did many kitten-like things.
She tangled with kites,
And took long, lazy flights
After anything airborne that sings.

There once was a cat who could fly
And was frequently seen in the sky
Chasing bees, bats, and more,
Hunting birds by the score,
Even stalking the angels on high!

LAWRENCE J. LEVINE

What do poets say about the relationship of
God and cats? Here's one view, from an
early nineteenth century German author—

Songs of Creation

God at first the sun created,
Then each nightly constellation;
From the sweat of his own forehead
Oxen were his next creation.

Wild beasts he created later,
Lions with their paws so furious;
In the image of the lion
Made he kittens small and curious. . . .

Henrich Heine

$\mathcal{I}$f God created man in his own image,
you've got to wonder: in whose image did
He create the nobler cat?

Unknown

ANGEL OF THE NIGHT

I know my cat's an angel
For she watches over me.
Slyly, when her eyes seem shut;
At night, when I can't see.

I know my cat's an angel
For her ears protect my sleep.
A creak, a squeak, a footfall;
At any noise she'll leap.

I know my cat's an angel
For she curls up at my side;
A warning to intruders
That it's best to run and hide.

I know my cat's an angel
For although she hasn't wings
I'm safe and warm beside her,
Wrapped in all the love she brings.

NANCY JOSEPH

Cats can be angels, but they can also be gods.

In Ancient Egypt, cats were kept to kill the mice and rats that attacked grain storage bins. Early Egyptians believed that cats were sent by the gods to protect them, and treated them accordingly. They were fed bread soaked in milk and fish from the Nile. Anyone who killed a cat, even accidentally, was put to death.

In time, Egyptians decided that the cats themselves were gods. The cult of the cat goddess Bast originated in the Nile Delta some time before 950 B.C. and flourished for nearly two thousand years. Bast was also known as Bastet or Pasht, from which our word "pussy" comes.

Bast personified the kinder aspects of the cat. She was a goddess of pleasure, music, and dance, and pilgrims came from all over to worship in her temple. Their approach was typically accompanied by music, singing, and dancing. Bast was also goddess of the night, since cats moved about when other animals rested.

The seat of Bast's cult was the city of Bubastis, the one-time capital of Egypt.

Bast was generally pictured as a human female with a cat's head, though she was also portrayed as a giant cat. In her cat-form, she typically wore gold earrings and a gold nose-ring.

What kind of pets do you suppose angels have? A stand-up comic takes a serious look at the question:

Can you imagine an angel—
Walking a dog?
Feeding a goldfish?
Riding a horse?
Keeping an ant farm or apiary?
Hammering together a hutch?
Being amused by a parrot's voice or the tiny wings of a canary?
Or can you imagine an angel—
Celestial and radiant with a kitten curled at its feet or in its lap?
While there is surely a place in Heaven for all God's creatures,
    the cat has a special place in the order of things.

Norman Klar

Then there are those who mistakenly believe that cats are demons in disguise who serve witches and warlocks and other practitioners of the black arts. One early twentieth-century poet suggests that cats hang around with witches with instructions from above, God's special forces:

I have often heard it said that
The witch-familiar is a cat.
This may be true of a black bat
Even more so of a big rat.
But I believe God gave a pat
To puss and said, "Sit by the vat."
So each cat now curls on her mat,
Alert to swat the witch's hat.

Rose Epstein

Instead of pews,
Cats pray in mews.
C. B. Bone

THE CAT

The cat
One night was very bored.
The cat
Behaving most untoward,
The cat
Saw dog, a pail, and poured.
The cat
And dog together warred:
The cat
In combat grave was gored.
The cat
He died, to heaven soar'd.
The cat
He brushed God's flaming sword.
The cat
He said, "May I stay, Lord?"
The cat
Was told, "Yes. You're Adored."
The cat
Curled up and soon he snored.
The dog
On earth was truly floored.

Michael Schneider

In this work, a familiar story is embellished with
what we all know is certainly the truth—

The Gospel of the Holy Twelve

And Joseph with Mary also went up from Galilee, out of the city of Nazareth into Judaea, unto the city of David, which is called Bethlehem (because they were of the house and lineage of David), to be taxed with Mary his espoused wife, who was great with child.

And so it was, that while they were there, the days were accomplished that she should be delivered. And she brought forth her firstborn child in a Cave, and wrapped him in swaddling clothes, and laid him in a manger, which was in the cave; because there was no room for them in the inn. And behold it was filled with many lights, bright as the Sun in his glory.

And there were in the same cave an ox, and a horse, and an ass and a sheep, and beneath the manger was a cat with her little ones.

Gideon Ousley

What of cats who are not yet angels?
Are they secretly devout? They are,
according to—

A KITTEN IN CHURCH

I have only once seen a pussy in church. It was not a parish church, but the chapel of one of the great London hospitals. The congregation was assembled and was awaiting the entrance of the chaplain, when a young pussy of an age somewhere between cat and kitten solemnly marched with tail erect, up the middle gangway. Without hesitation, and as if fulfilling a usual duty, he made for the reading desk, entered it, and for an instant was lost to view. But a moment later head and shoulder appeared above the desk, and a small wise face looked round with an air of quiet assurance and professional unconcern. I quite expected to see the little paws reverently folded, and to hear a tiny voice say: 'Let us purr'!

Gertrude Jekyll

Is there a place in Heaven for cats?
Some authors are convinced of it!

A Traffic Martyr

His coat was partly black as ink,
And partly white as snow
When it was clean, and that is why
We called him 'Domino'.

He came from nowhere suddenly,
And claimed us all as friends,
And as he wasn't anyone's
He lived on odds and ends.

But little Domino is dead,
A big wheel squashed him flat,
And with him died the sweetest thing
That only was a cat

He's gone where all the kittens go
That are too good for earth,
The Paradise of little cats
And puppies drowned at birth.

SIR EDWARD DENNISON ROSS

Though many cats of European legend are wicked, there *are* exceptions. One, in fact.

The Cailleach Bheur of the Scottish Highlands was a goddess who took the form of a cat. In this form, she herded deer in the autumn to bring them to pockets of food. But still the playful kitty, she also clawed her way onto the trees to knock dead leaves from the branches.

Angel or Devil?

I always believed that my Himalayan was angelic, a loving face set in a cloud of white fleece, dark ears forming a proud halo, the gentlest of cat voices.

Then I saw it catch a mouse. And the fleece turned red, and the ears became horns, that sweet voice hissed like the Serpent himself, and my angel was the devil incarnate!

Dr. Orlito Trias

$\mathcal{I}$ know that God is depressed and
needs cheering. Why else take this
kitten I cherish so?

Epitaph in a Pet Cemetery

Mice can be found with some regularity
in the pages of the Bible, but not cats.
Is there a reason for this?

C ats aren't mentioned anywhere in the
Bible, which may have to do with their
importance, as deities, to the Egyptians.
On the other hand, there are a number of
dogs in the Bible, which might also explain
their absence.

CHARLTON HESTON

*C*ats born in spring
The devil bring.
Cats born in fall
Are angels all.

New England folklore

According to an old European folktale, when cats were first created they had wings. But they preyed on birds and threatened them with extinction. So God took away the cats' wings—though he turned their flutter into a purr, reminding kittens of the time and form in which they were most content.

*G*od made the cat to give man the pleasure of petting the tiger.

FRANCOIS MERY

What looks like a cat angel, sounds like a cat angel, and is equally fanciful?

I have always felt that a cat and a nightingaie combined would make the most perfect creature, winging its melodious way through the night.

DIANA HARRYHAUSEN

Some cats didn't stay in the afterworld long enough to be considered angels.

As far back as the fifth century A.D., both Chinese and Japanese mystics believed that good people were reincarnated, not as people but as cats. That is why, when cats showed up on doorsteps, they were taken in and pampered.

Many Buddhist and Hindu sects believe that going from human to cat is a step forward in achieving Nirvana, a state of perfect freedom from pain and worry.

What is it about these animals that makes a hellcat easy to imagine while an angelcat seems like an oxymoron?

CHARLES SCHNEER

My cat has what appears to be the silhouette of an angel in the black-and-white markings of her fur—the kind of angel children make in the snow by lying on their backs and waving their arms.

The angel wasn't there when I got her as a kitten, and I suspect this is her little medal for being a good influence on me.

ARNOLD BELNICK

From *Mother Goosed* (unpublished), comes this
bit of doggerel . . . or should that be caterel?

Hey diddle diddle, the cat and the fiddle
Were resting upon an escarp.
Before she bestirred,
A landslide occurred.
Now the kitty is playing a harp.

Sam Calvin

It isn't necessary for cats to have wings and a halo to be thought of as angels. Most cats achieve seraphic virtue through the love they give.

Authors, poets, and essayists have described this pure, God-given affection in many different ways:

I love cats because I love my home, and little by little they become its visible soul.

Jean Cocteau

*A*ll your wondrous wealth of hair;
Dark and fair,
Silken-shaggy, soft and bright
As the clouds and beams of night,
Pays my reverent hand's caress
Back with friendlier gentleness.

Algernon Charles Swinburne

For I will consider my Cat Jeoffry.
For he is the servant of the Living God,
    duly and daily serving him.
For at the first glance of the glory of God
    in the East he worships in his way.

For this is done by wreathing his body seven
    times round with elegant quickness.
For then he leaps up to catch the musk,
    which is the blessing of God upon
    his prayer.
For he rolls upon prank to work it in.
For having done duty and received blessing
    he begins to consider himself.

Christopher Smart

This fun, slightly irreverent bit of verse suggests that while you can dress a cat up in angel's robes, you can't necessarily change its nature!

THE CHOICE

He meets the cats at Heaven's door
And bids them enter, rich or poor.

He welcomes them with arms spread wide
Then bends close to them, once inside.

And says to them, "It's Heaven's law:
You do not hiss, show teeth or claw.

For mice and bird, 'tis Heaven too.
You don't give chase, you don't say 'boo!'

Most cats regard Him long and well
And say, "I'd rather go——"

Ah, well!

JOHN QUIRK

*W*ho can believe that there is no soul
behind those luminous eyes!

Theophile Gautier

EPITAPH

Here lies Belaud, my little gray cat:
Belaud, that was the most handsome perhaps
That Nature ever made in cat's clothing:
This was Belaud, Death to Rats,
Belaud, to be sure his beauty was such
That he deserves to be immortal

JOACHIM DU BALLAY

Thoughts on a Cat Ghost

Would a black cat become a white ghost?
Would a ghost cat go "boo" or "meoo"?
Would the hem of a cat ghost's sheet be its legs or its tail?
Would a cat ghost chase ghost mice or real mice?
Would a ghostly cat rub against your leg or
float up and rub your head?

David George

ODE ON THE DEATH OF A FAVOURITE CAT DROWNED IN A TUB OF GOLD FISHES

'Twas on a lofty vase's side
    Where China's gayest art had dyed
    The azure flowers, that blow;
Demurest of the tabby kind,
The pensive Selima, reclined,
    Gazed on the lake below.

Her conscious tail her joy declared;
The fair round face, the snowy beard,
    The velvet of her paws,
Her coat, that with the tortoise vies,
Her ears of jet, and emerald eyes,
    She saw; and purr'd applause.

Still had she gazed; but 'midst the tide
Two angel forms were seen to glide,
    The genii of the stream:
Their scaly armour's Tyrian hue
Through richest purple to the view
    Betray'd a golden gleam.

The hapless nymph with wonder saw:
A whisker first, and then a claw,
  With many an ardent wish,
She stretch'd, in vain, to reach the prize
What female heart can gold despise?
  What cat's averse to fish?

Presumptuous maid! with looks intent
Again she stretch'd, again she bent,
  Nor knew the gulf between.
(Malignant Fate sat by, and smiled)
The slipp'ry verge her feet beguiled,
  She tumbled headlong in.

Eight times emerging from the flood
She mew'd to ev'ry wat'ry God,
    Some speedy aid to send.
No Dolphin came, no Nereid stirr'd:
Nor cruel Tom, nor Susan heard.
    A fav'rite has no friend!

From hence, ye beauties, undeceived,
Know, one false step is ne'er retrieved,
    And be with caution bold.
Not all that tempts your wand'ring eyes
And heedless hearts is lawful prize.
    Nor all that glitters, gold.

THOMAS GRAY

In Norse mythology, the cat was the special animal of Freyja, the Scandinavian goddess of fertility, beauty, love, and marriage. In this capacity—the equivalent of a Judeo-Christian angel—cats were responsible for drawing her chariot through the skies.

It was considered good luck to get married on her namesake day, Friday, since this guaranteed fertility for the newlyweds.

Cats and lions were sacred in Ancient China, presumed to have the power to repel evil with a glance or roar, respectively, and to protect crops from predators. These animals were sometimes pictured with wings, as befitted their celestial status.

As lions became extinct, the Chinese bred Pekingese dogs to resemble them and take their place in the holy pantheon.

A well-known athlete/actor once reminisced about how he reformed a devilish kitty into an angel on a film location:

The cat was named Angelpuss, though it seemed that only the latter half of the name applied. She would charge down the dark hallway, her eyes aglow like green coals, her ears pointed devilishly. She would hide behind a door and swat at my foot as I walked by. At other times, she would ignore me as if I were contemptible.

One day, I went for a swim in the pool. She came forward, curious, so I gave her a splash. She ran off, leaving wet little paw-prints on the concrete. After that, though, she was very well behaved around me—very much the Angelpuss.

Buster Crabbe

In 1921, Kraken, the cat belonging to Captain Sterling Hammer of the schooner *Nancy Hanks*, jumped into the berth of its sleeping master. The animal was mewing and wailing frantically, and when the captain woke he found thick, dark smoke churning from below the deck.

Sounding the bell and waking the crew, Captain Hammer was able to evacuate all hands safely. Amid all the confusion, the cat vanished. Only later did the captain find its body in the hold where the fire had started.

The cat had been pinned under a falling crate and asphixiated almost at once, several minutes before its spirit appeared to rouse its master.

I think I know why cats horde yarn balls. It's so that when they die, they'll be able to climb back to earth if Heaven's too dull.

D. J. Schow

This saying among the Welsh pertained to people on their deathbed:

Spy a black cat last
And in hell you'll reside.
Spy a white cat last
And to Heaven you'll fly.

*I*f cats were allowed in Heaven,
wouldn't we see all these tails hanging
down through the clouds?

Diane Albright

On the wall of the old Yankee Doodle Inn, late of Norwalk, CT, the following saw was displayed:

If a cat washes its face from cheek to ear
Your guardian angel she'll be for a year.
If a cat does its cleaning from ear to cheek
Bad luck you will have for the following week.

A number of saws and poems warn that May is an unlucky time for cats to be born. This short verse suggests that the cats of May become angels quicker than most:

May-born cats don't hunt down rats;
Don't run from dogs that bite; are nice.
Heaven's full of May-born cats.
I'd rather it be full of mice.

Anonymous

EPITAPH

Ashes to ashes,
Dust to dust.
Kitty's in Heaven,
That hound dog be cussed!

*T*he angel cat, 'neath folded wings,
Sat down with harp and plucked its strings.
Instead of harp-sounds pure and true,
The instrument sang, "Mew, mew, mew!"
Timothy Moriarty

According to lore attributed to the Dutch, only on Christmas Eve, and then in private, do cats get on their knees, fold their paws together, shut their eyes, and pray.

It isn't known what they pray for, though legend has it that they get what they wish—which is why not a creature is stirring on that night, "not even a mouse."

I Know Why Cats Don't Like Water

The answer's plain as it could be:
Why cats do not like rain,
Or hoses, streams, or sparkling sea,
Or tubs with stoppered drain.

I found out when my cat and I
Got caught in such a storm.
The droplets showed quite clear—oh my!—
An unexpected form.

Two hazy wings with feathers small,
A halo gold and high.
There was no doubt, no none at all,
Why kittens must stay dry.

Next time you look in pussy's eyes
You'll see it in plain view:
They're heaven's angels in disguise,
Here on earth to bless you.

CINDY MERRITT

Pussycat, Pussycat fly away
Run on beams of sunlight.
Hunt with the hawks and chase clouds all day
And rue the fall of night.

Nursery Rhyme

A cat can't enter heaven or hell
unless it has used all of its nine lives.

American lore

In many Native American cultures, cats had powers of life and death corresponding to those of the Egyptian god Bast. Warriors wearing cat masks would partake in ceremonies, hoping that the spirit of dead cats would enter their bodies and give them feline stealth and cunning.

One of the holiest cats in history was Meuzza, which belonged to Mohammed. According to legend, the prophet was called to prayer one day. The cat was asleep on his arm and, rather than wake it, Mohammed cut the sleeve from his robe and set it down with the dozing cat.

The blessed cat resides in Paradise.

According to the Koran, the cat is the essence of purity. A cat hospital was built in Bab-el-Nasz, and it was considered a blessing to bring food to the patients.

It is unlawful to chase cats from mosques.

An Avenging Angel

The most famous "ghost" cat in literature is "The Black Cat" in the short story by Edgar Allen Poe (1809–1849).

A man and his new bride procure a black cat named Pluto, which they adore. Years later, the hero —now an alcoholic—hangs the cat. That night, the house burns down, the man and his wife barely escaping with their lives.

The couple acquire a new cat which, in time, begins to display the white outline of a noose on its black fur. Convinced the cat is haunted, the narrator attempts to kill it with an axe but strikes his wife instead. He buries her in the wall of the house and is surprised and delighted to find that the cat has vanished. The police arrive days later: crying from within the wall—where it, too, had been walled-in — the cat leads them to the corpse.

If God created animal angels, they would
probably be dogs. Cats would
consider it a demotion.

LINDA MARROW

The Chinese philosopher Confucius owned a cat and always kept it by his side. He apparently believed that the cat was sent from heaven to serve as a conduit for divine wisdom.

A Lament

She's gone where all good kittens go
When life's short work is done.
My Nubbelles, with her eyes aglow,
Face sweet, second-to-none.
I'll miss the softness of her fur,
Her purring in the den.
I hope an angel cares for her
Until we're joined again.

Charlotte Abram

*G*od is probably a 'cat person.'
After a day of listening to supplicants try
to please Him, He probably wouldn't
want a dog around.

John Ritter

I f a cat had a halo, it would probably
wear it around its tail. It makes
a statement.

Sergio Aragones

A cat's idea of heaven would be
mice from wall to wall.
A mouse's view of heaven would be
no cats there at all.

Andrea Stempel

Her voice like a harp, her fur soft as a cloud,
Eyes bright as the sun, her head high and unbowed.
I asked my dear kitty, so small but so proud,
"Are you an angel?" She just smiled and meowed.

Harleigh Kidd